WHAT ARE SUPPLY AND DEMAND?

LAURA LA BELLA

Britannica®
Educational Publishing

IN ASSOCIATION WITH

ROSEN
EDUCATIONAL SERVICES

Published in 2017 by Britannica Educational Publishing (a trademark of Encyclopædia Britannica, Inc.) in association with The Rosen Publishing Group, Inc.
29 East 21st Street, New York, NY 10010

Distributed exclusively by Rosen Publishing.

To see additional Britannica Educational Publishing titles, go to rosenpublishing.com.

First Edition

Britannica Educational Publishing
J.E. Luebering: Executive Director, Core Editorial
Mary Rose McCudden: Editor, Britannica Student Encyclopedia

Rosen Publishing
Heather Moore Niver: Editor
Nelson Sá: Art Director
Brian Garvey: Designer
Cindy Reiman: Photography Manager
Heather Moore Niver: Photo Researcher

Library of Congress Cataloging-in-Publication Data

Names: La Bella, Laura, author.
Title: What is supply and demand? / Laura La Bella.
Description: First Edition. | New York : Britannica Educational Publishing,
  2017. | Series: Let's find out! Community economics | Includes bibliographical
  references and index.
Identifiers: LCCN 2016001000| ISBN 9781680484069 (library bound : alk. paper)
  | ISBN 9781680484144 (pbk. : alk. paper) | ISBN 9781680483826 (6-pack :
  alk. paper)
Subjects: LCSH: Supply and demand--Juvenile literature.
Classification: LCC HB801 .L213 2017 | DDC 338.5/21--dc23
LC record available at http://lccn.loc.gov/2016001000

Manufactured in the United States of America

Photo Credits: Cover, interior pages background image © iStockphoto.com/kupico; pp. 4, 27 Fuse/Thinkstock; p. 5 Chip Somodevilla/Getty Images; p. 6 shironosov/iStock/Thinkstock; p. 7 © iStockphoto.com/arturbo; p. 8 TanawatPontchour/iStock/Thinkstock; p. 9 pressdigital/iStock/Thinkstock; p. 10 Hatchapong Palurtchaivong/ Shutterstock.com; p. 11 Michael Mauney/The LIFE Images Collection/Getty Images; p. 12 © iStockphoto.com/ PeopleImages; p. 13 © iStockphoto.com/JohnCarnemolla; p. 14 amlanmathur/iStock/Thinkstock; p. 15 ullstein bild/ Getty Images; p. 16 alrisha/iStock/Thinkstock; p. 17 Bloomberg/Getty Images; p. 18 © iStockphoto.com/Rawpixel Ltd; p. 19 mongione/Shutterstock.com; p. 20 © iStockphoto.com/4FR; p. 21 © iStockphoto.com/MickyWiswedel; p. 22 thitivong/iStock/Thinkstock; pp. 22-23 grapestock/iStock/Thinkstock; p. 24 grinvalds/iStock/Thinkstock; p. 25 razyph/ iStock/Thinkstock; p. 26 sakkmesterke/iStock/Thinkstock; p. 28 Design Pics/Thinkstock; p. 29 Lisa S./Shutterstock.com

CONTENTS

An Overview of Supply and Demand

An economy is made up of producers and consumers. Producers make or provide goods and services. Consumers in turn are the people who pay for and use those goods and services.

Every time we shop we become consumers, or people who buy goods and services.

The amount of goods consumers want to buy is called demand. The amount companies produce is called supply.

The relationship between supply and demand helps set the prices for the goods and services.

If there is a large supply of an item and the demand for the item is low, the price will be low. If there is a small supply and a high demand, the price will be high. For example, suppose there is a new toy that everyone wants. If the producer only made a few, consumers will pay a high price to make sure they can get one of those few.

COMPARE AND CONTRAST

What are the differences between consumers and producers? How do consumers and producers each have an effect on the economy?

The BB-8™ Droid from the movie *Star Wars: The Force Awakens* was a popular toy in late 2015, which created a strong demand.

GOODS AND SERVICES

Supply and demand refers to the availability of goods

and services. A good is an object that people can touch or hold, such as food, clothing, video games, cell phones, and books. Some producers

Goods, like books, toys, and other items, are objects you can hold, feel, and touch.

Services are actions a person does for someone else, such as teaching swimming lessons.

manufacture goods, such as clothing and video game systems. Other goods, such as fruits and vegetables, are grown. A service is an action that a person does for someone else. Hairstylists, car mechanics, teachers, and swimming instructors are all people who offer services. Some businesses, such as restaurants, provide both goods and services. They provide food as well as people to serve the food.

To **manufacture** something means to take raw materials and make them into a product either by hand or by using machines.

Producing Goods and Services

Producers create goods and provide services. They grow things on a farm, make things by hand or in a factory, or provide services. A producer can be an individual person or a company. Many goods are made from natural resources, such as wood, which

A **company** is a group of people working together to produce goods or services.

Goods can be grown, manufactured by a company, or handmade, such as jewelry or pottery.

comes from trees. Wood is used to manufacture pencils, paper, books, furniture, toys, and more. Some goods that are grown, such as cotton, are sold to producers,

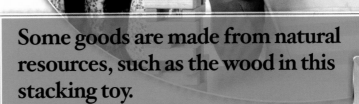

Some goods are made from natural resources, such as the wood in this stacking toy.

who use them to make other goods.

Producers make goods and services in response to demand from consumers for a particular item. The more in demand a product is, the more a producer may make to fulfill the demand. The demand will also influence the price of the item. If there is a great demand for a product, the price will go up.

PLANNING AND RESEARCH

Producers must plan ahead when they think about making a product or providing a service. To do that, they have to think about both supply and demand.

Before they make a product or provide a service, they have to know whether there is a demand for the product or the service. The demand is what people want and

Needs are things you cannot live without, such as water, shelter, and food.

Wants are treats, like ice cream, or items that you can live without, such as video game consoles.

need. Wants are not the same as needs. Needs are things that people must have in order to survive. Food, shelter, water, and clothing are needs. Wants are things that people would like to have but do not need. Toys, televisions, jewelry, and candy are wants.

COMPARE AND CONTRAST

Think about the things a person needs to survive and the items a person wants. What are the differences? How do needs and wants affect supply and demand?

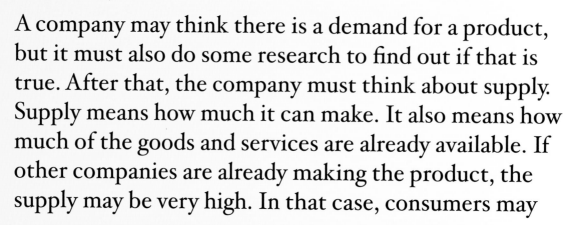

A company may think there is a demand for a product, but it must also do some research to find out if that is true. After that, the company must think about supply. Supply means how much it can make. It also means how much of the goods and services are already available. If other companies are already making the product, the supply may be very high. In that case, consumers may not pay as much for the product.

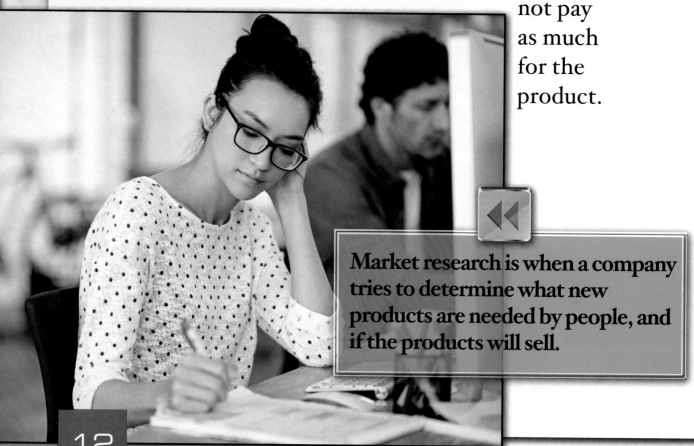

Market research is when a company tries to determine what new products are needed by people, and if the products will sell.

Companies want to make money, so they need to think about how much consumers will pay for a product. Companies also need to think about how much it will cost them to make a product. That cost includes paying for the raw materials that go into the product. It also includes paying the workers who make and sell the product.

THINK ABOUT IT

If a restaurant knows there is going to be a big event one week, how can thinking about supply and demand help the owner prepare for that?

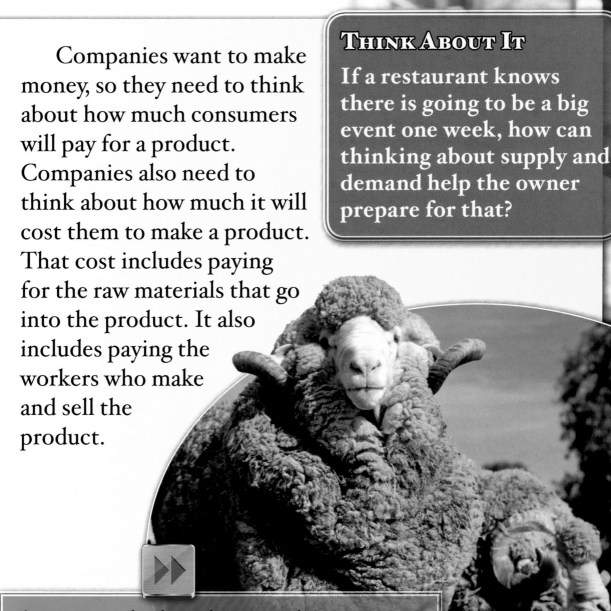

A company looks at how much it costs to make a product. It looks at the price of necessary raw materials, such as wool.

RESOURCES

Producers have to think about the raw materials they need to make a product. Raw materials can be things like paper, glue, paint, and string to make a kite or electronic parts and plastic to make a video game. If there are plenty of materials available, a producer can make many goods. If the materials are not easy to get, the producer cannot

If raw materials, such as the paper, glue, and string used to make kites, are easy to get, a product can be made easily.

Think About It

Natural resources are limited. What would happen if we do not monitor and manage how natural resources are used? How do you think this might affect the production of goods and services?

create a supply or will have to charge more for the product.

Rare earth elements are expensive and can increase the price of a product. They could also limit how many items can be produced.

Often the raw materials are things known as natural resources. A natural resource is something of value people get from the environment, such as air, water, plants, animals, rocks, and minerals. Some resources are renewable, which means they can be replaced or grown back. Trees are a renewable resource. Wood is used to make paper, furniture, houses, toys, and more. New trees can be planted and more

Trees can be planted and deforestation can be managed. This makes trees a renewable resource.

Nonrenewable resources cannot be easily replaced. It can take millions of years for coal, oil, and other nonrenewable resources to form.

can be grown in a short amount of time. Nonrenewable resources cannot be replaced or they take a very long time to be replaced or grow back. Fossil fuels are nonrenewable natural resources. They cannot be easily replaced.

Fossil fuels are sources of energy that took millions of years to form. They include petroleum (oil), coal, and natural gas.

LABOR

Labor is the workers who make goods and provide services. It is the most expensive cost for a producer. A producer must control how many workers it employs and how much it pays them.

> To **employ** means to use or to provide someone with a job and to pay them for their work.

When a company sells a product it must take away the cost of the labor and resources that it spent to make the product. Whatever is left is

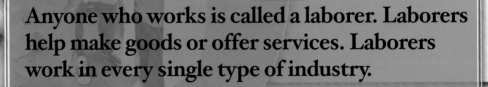

Anyone who works is called a laborer. Laborers help make goods or offer services. Laborers work in every single type of industry.

Much thought needs to go into how many pairs of jeans can be manufactured each day for a company to earn a profit.

called a profit. For example, if a company charges $30.00 for a pair of jeans, it does not make a profit of $30.00. It must pay for the material and the thread that was used to make the jeans. It must also pay for the workers who sewed the jeans. If the material cost is $5.00 and the labor cost is $15.00 for each pair of jeans, the profit equals $10.00.

Suppose a factory that makes jeans has three workers and three sewing machines. Together the three workers can make 12 pairs of jeans each day. If the owner of the factory hires one more worker, the company can make 16 pairs of jeans. The company can now produce a larger supply of jeans. If it

COMPARE AND CONTRAST

How are workers and resources similar? How are they different?

Factories make all sorts of goods—from clothing and furniture to toys and electronics.

Workers who are skilled in sewing are often employed in clothing factories. They can make everything from shirts to outerwear.

charges the same amount for each pair of jeans, it will make more money by producing 16 pairs.

However, the company has to pay each worker a salary. The salary for the extra worker may be more than the extra money the company makes by selling the extra pairs of jeans.

INTERNATIONAL TRADE

International trade is the business of buying and selling goods and services between nations. The citizens of one country may want goods they do not have the resources to make. Under these conditions, countries look elsewhere to find what they need. Some countries sell products to others. These products are called exports. Other

Countries often import some goods and services and export other goods and services.

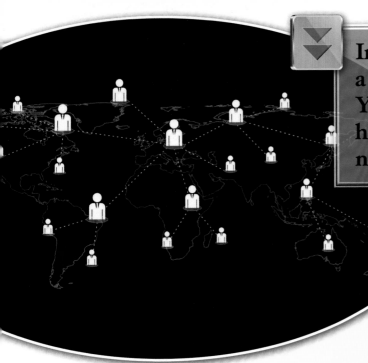

International trade is part of a process called globalization. Your purchase locally may help support families living in nations around the world.

countries buy items from other nations. These items are called imports. International trade affects the supply and demand in both the country that makes the goods and the country that buys the goods. In some cases a product may be made in more than one country. However, one country may be able to make it for less money.

In that case, there may be a greater supply of the product at a lower cost. That will increase demand.

THINK ABOUT IT

Is it better for a country to have more exports than imports or more imports than exports? Which ones bring money into a country?

MICROECONOMICS AND MACROECONOMICS

Economics is the study of how people make goods and services and how others pay for those goods and services. There are two main branches of economics. Microeconomics looks at individual consumers and businesses.

Macroeconomics is the study of how a whole country's economy works. People who study microeconomics try to explain why consumers

People who study economics seek to understand how and why consumers buy one product over another.

buy one product rather than another. They also look at why companies choose to produce one good or service instead of another. Another area of study is the relationship of

Microeconomics is the study of businesses and consumers at a local level.

workers and their employers.

Microeconomics can help explain how a neighborhood sandwich shop sets the prices of its products and how that will affect the shop's business.

COMPARE AND CONTRAST

How are microeconomics and macroeconomics similar? How are they different?

People who study macroeconomics look at the value of all the goods and services that a country produces. They also study economic growth, or how a nation's wealth becomes larger. Economists look at how people create wealth, how they use it, and how different people get different amounts of it.

> **Value** is the amount of money something is worth.

Governments are interested in macroeconomics as well. A government plays an important role in its country's economy. In some countries, the government decides which

Economists study the entire buying and selling environment to understand where money is being created, spent, and used.

goods and services should be produced and sold. It also decides how many goods should be produced and sets the prices for the goods. This is called a planned economy.

By contrast, most governments let companies and consumers decide what will be produced. This is called a free market.

In a free-market economy a company can decide for itself what products and services it will provide for consumers.

UNLIMITED WANTS, LIMITED RESOURCES

You make decisions about your needs and wants every day. You decide what to eat, what to wear, and what games to play. You also decide what you want to buy. You can't have all of the things you want all of the time, so you have to make choices. Yours and everyone else's decisions affect the economy as a whole.

You are a key part of the supply and demand process. Everyone's wants and needs are taken into account. They affect the entire economy.

Producers have to make choices as well. They must decide how to use the available resources to make products that people will want to buy. They hope that the supply they provide matches the demand from consumers.

THINK ABOUT IT

Sometimes there are not enough resources to fulfill a need. How do you think limited resources affect which goods and services are produced?

Producers help decide what items to sell each day. They want to make sure they supply enough to meet their customers' demands.

GLOSSARY

consumer A person who buys and uses up goods.

economics The study of the production and use of goods and services.

export A product or service that is created in one country and sent to another country to be sold.

import A product or service that is brought into a country from another country.

international Involving two or more nations.

manufacture To create something out of raw materials.

market A meeting together of people to buy and sell.

production The act or process of producing or making something.

profit The gain or benefit from something. In economics, the money that a business keeps after paying costs.

society A system or group of living things that depend on each other and usually form a social unit.

trade To take part in the exchange, purchase, or sale of goods.

For More Information

Books

Balconi, Michelle A., Dr. Arthur Laffer, and Mary Kinsora. *Let's Chat About Economics!: Basic Principles Through Everyday Scenarios.* New York, NY: Gichigami Press, Inc., 2014.

Challen, Paul, and Gare Thompson. *What Is Supply and Demand?* St. Catharines, ON: Crabtree Publishing Company, 2010.

Larson, Jennifer S. *What Can You Do With Money?: Earning, Spending and Saving.* Minneapolis, MN: Lerner Publishing Group, 2010.

Larson, Jennifer S. *Who's Buying? Who's Selling?: Understanding Consumers and Producers.* Minneapolis, MN: Lerner Publishing Group, 2010.

Nelson, Robin. *What Do We Buy?: A Look at Goods and Services.* Minneapolis, MN: Lerner Classroom, 2010.

Websites

Because of the changing nature of Internet links, Rosen Publishing has developed an online list of websites related to the subject of this book. This site is updated regularly. Please use this link to access the list:

http://www.rosenlinks.com/ LFO/supp

INDEX